Exploring the Unknown

The Extinction of the Dinosaurs

by Don Nardo

Lucent Books, P.O. 289011, San Diego, CA 92198-9011

These and other titles are included in the Exploring the Unknown series:

> The Curse of Tutankhamen
> The Extinction of the Dinosaurs
> Haunted Houses

Library of Congress Cataloging-in-Publication Data
Nardo, Don, 1947–
    The extinction of the dinosaurs / by Don Nardo.
      p. cm.—(Exloring the Unknown)
      Includes bibliographical references and index.
      Summary: Explores the many contradictory theories about what caused the dinosaurs to become extinct.
      ISBN 1-56006-154-5 (alk. paper)
      1. Dinosaurs—Juvenile literature. [1. Dinosaurs. 2. Extinction (Biology)] I. Title. II. Series: Exploring the unknown (San Diego, Calif.)
QE862.D5N37   1994
567.9'1—dc20
                                      93–4314
                                        CIP
                                        AC

C O N T E N T S

INTRODUCTION

The air is warm and moist on a late afternoon some sixty-five million years ago. Huge reptiles roam through a lush jungle landscape near the shore of a shallow sea. A giant beast quietly nibbles the top branches of a palm tree. Without warning a pack of bloodthirsty meat eaters attacks. They savagely tear hunks of flesh out of the larger reptile. Terrified by the sounds of the struggle, other plant eaters run into a nearby swamp. There, several large reptiles take menacing stances. They guard their eggs, which rest in crude nests dug in the mud.

Suddenly a brilliant light flashes across the sky. Many of the great reptiles flinch in surprise. A few minutes later the ground lurches violently. It begins to heave back and forth. A deafening roar immediately follows. It throws animals of all kinds into a state of confusion and panic. The sky quickly grows pitch black. Huge bolts of lightning rip through the darkness. Gigantic waves rush in from the sea. They crush and drown the creatures living near the shore. The darkness continues for days and the air turns cold. Days stretch into weeks and weeks into months. Most of the plants die. So do the huge land and sea reptiles that depend on them for food. When the sunlight finally returns, all the great beasts are dead.

Is this how the dinosaurs died? Many scientists think it is. They believe that a large comet struck the earth. They think it caused a disaster all around the world. Only some mammals and other small animals survived. Other scientists disagree They say the dinosaurs died more gradually. Some researche

Animals of the late Cretaceous browse, unaware of their approaching doom.

believe changes in climate caused the end of these beasts. Others say the dinosaurs died from eating poisonous plants. Scientists have suggested many other theories as well. All around the world they search for evidence for these theories. They want to solve, once and for all, one of the greatest riddles of science: the strange disappearance of the dinosaurs.

CHAPTER 1

In the Days of the Dinosaurs

One day in 1822, quite by accident, Mary Mantell made one of the most important discoveries in the history of science. She was standing on a road in southern England waiting for her husband, Gideon Mantell. Suddenly she noticed a strange object in the gravel on the roadside. It appeared to be a large tooth. Excitedly, she showed the tooth to her husband, who was an English country doctor. She knew he would be interested because his hobby was collecting fossils. Fossils are the remains of long-dead plants and animals.

For a long time the tooth puzzled Dr. Mantell. It did not seem to belong to any known animal. At that time scientists believed the world's living creatures were the only kinds of animals that had ever existed. The idea that unknown animals had once existed and then died out thrilled and fascinated Mantell. Eventually he decided the tooth looked very much like those of a common iguana lizard. So he named the fossil *Iguanodon,* meaning "iguana tooth." But the teeth of modern lizards were only about a quarter of an inch long. The mystery tooth was more than three inches long! Mantell determined that the *Iguanodon* was an extremely large reptile that was extinct, or no longer existed.

In the following years people discovered many more teeth and bones of large extinct reptiles. Scientists eagerly studied these remains. They noticed many common features. The researchers all came to the same unusual and exciting conclusion that Mantell had: a large group of previously unknown creatures, many of gigantic size, once walked the earth!

An English doctor in the early 1800s was the first to notice the similarity between a three-inch fossilized tooth and the one-quarter-inch tooth of a common iguana. Dr. Gideon Mantell concluded that the large tooth was from a huge, no longer existing, reptile that he named Iguanodon.

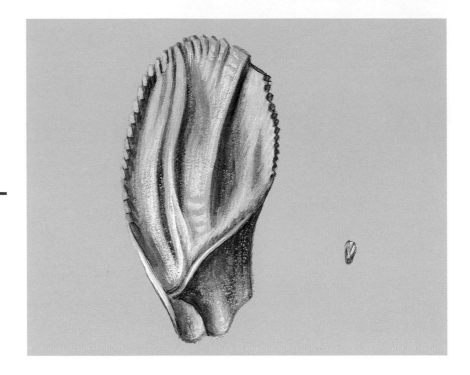

Dr. Gideon Mantell described the Iguanodon *in his book,* The Fossils of The South Downs, *published in 1822.*

Naming the Beasts

In 1842 the English scientist Sir Richard Owen gave the newly discovered animals a name. He reasoned that the huge, extinct lizards must have been awesome, terrifying beasts. So he called them dinosaurs. This word is a combination of the Greek words *deinos,* meaning "terrible," and *sauros,* meaning "lizard."

Paleontology is a branch of science that studies the fossils. This word came from the Greek words *palaio,* meaning "ancient," *onta,* meaning "living things," and *logos,* meaning "study of." The field of paleontology grew quickly in the late 1800s and early 1900s. Universities, museums, and wealthy individuals launched many expeditions to search for dinosaur fossils.

One of the most famous fossil hunts took place in 1922 in the remote Gobi Desert. This vast wasteland is in Mongolia, north of China. American scientist Roy Chapman Andrews led the expedition. It crossed hundreds of miles of scorching sands and rugged mountains. The researchers were in constant danger from poisonous snakes and gangs of bandits. Still, they made a number of sensational finds. Among these were the skeletons of several species, or kinds, of dinosaurs completely new to science.

Perhaps the most exciting discovery made by the Andrews expedition was a group of nests. They contained the eggs of a small-beaked dinosaur called *Protoceratops*. The eggs were about the size of potatoes. Over the course of millions of years they had fossilized, or turned to stone. The small mounds of earth and mud that had held the fossilized eggs had eroded, or worn away. This erosion exposed the eggs to the researchers' view.

Archaeologists uncover the fossilized remains of a Tyrannosaurus rex. *Such digs around the world provided evidence that the huge lizards lived some sixty-five million years ago.*

Many Kinds of Dinosaurs

In the years that followed, expeditions found the remains of dinosaurs and other prehistoric creatures in many places. Africa, Europe, Canada, and the western part of the United States all had important finds. Paleontologists learned that dinosaurs were the dominant, or leading, life forms on land for many millions of years.

Scientists found that many different kinds of dinosaurs existed. Some were huge, like the *Apatosaurus* (originally called *Brontosaurus*). This creature had a thick body and extremely long tail and neck. It often reached a length of seventy feet. It weighed at least thirty tons—as much as four elephants! Other dinosaurs were quite small. For instance, *Compsognathus* was about the size of a chicken.

Dinosaurs also differed in their eating habits. Scientists could tell from the shape of teeth and other bones which

*Dinosaurs ranged in size from those as small as a chicken—*Compsognathus—*to those weighing as much as four elephants—*Apatosaurus.

Anatosaurus*   Tyrannosaurus rex**   Apatosau

dinosaurs ate plants and which ate meat. *Anatosaurus* (or *Trachodon*) was an *herbivore,* or plant eater. It had a large flat bill like a duck's. The bill contained up to one thousand small, flat teeth for chewing twigs, pine needles, and seeds. *Stegosaurus* was another large herbivore. It was about twenty-five feet long and had a body about the size of an elephant's. *Stegosaurus* had two rows of thin, bony plates running down its back. It probably spent much of its time munching on ferns and other plants.

By contrast, *Tyrannosaurus rex* was a *carnivore,* or meat eater. This monster stood nearly twenty feet tall. Its huge head had three-foot jaws. They were lined with razor-sharp teeth that were six inches long. A savage hunter, it stalked slower, gentler animals such as *Anatosaurus.* After catching its prey, *Tyrannosaurus* held on with its sharp claws. It tore out hunks of flesh with its lethal, or deadly, jaws. It was probably the largest predator, or hunter, that ever lived.

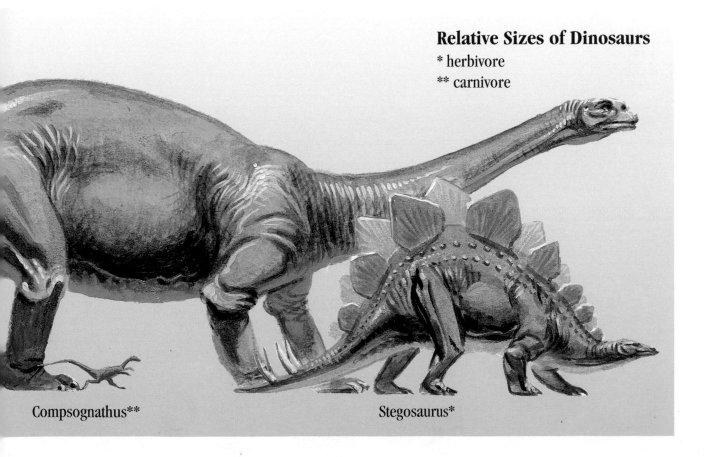

Relative Sizes of Dinosaurs
* herbivore
** carnivore

Compsognathus**   Stegosaurus*

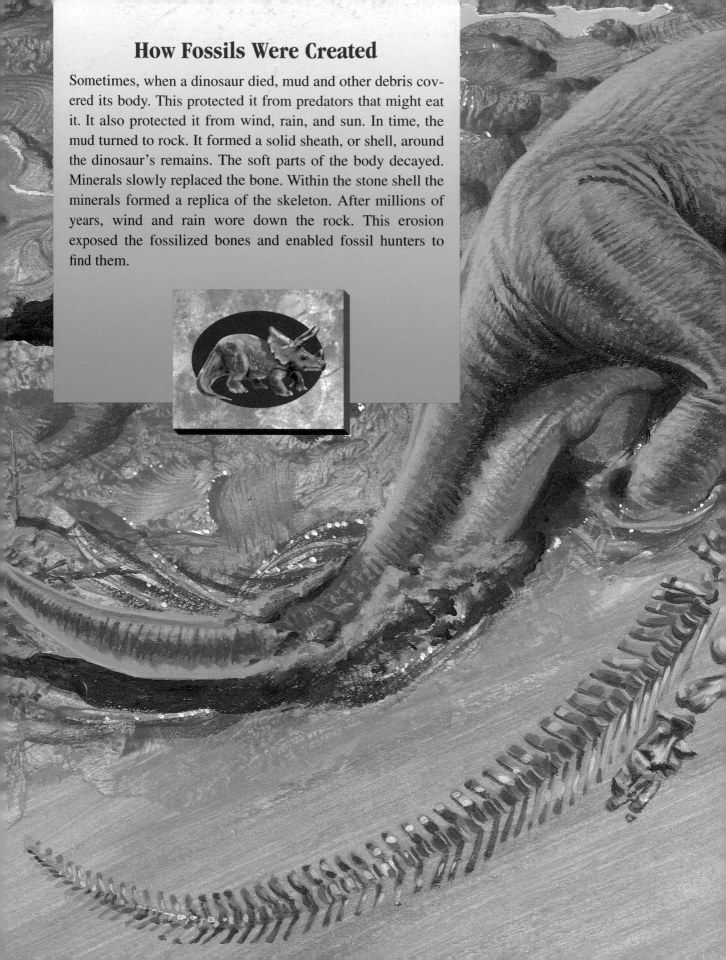

How Fossils Were Created

Sometimes, when a dinosaur died, mud and other debris covered its body. This protected it from predators that might eat it. It also protected it from wind, rain, and sun. In time, the mud turned to rock. It formed a solid sheath, or shell, around the dinosaur's remains. The soft parts of the body decayed. Minerals slowly replaced the bone. Within the stone shell the minerals formed a replica of the skeleton. After millions of years, wind and rain wore down the rock. This erosion exposed the fossilized bones and enabled fossil hunters to find them.

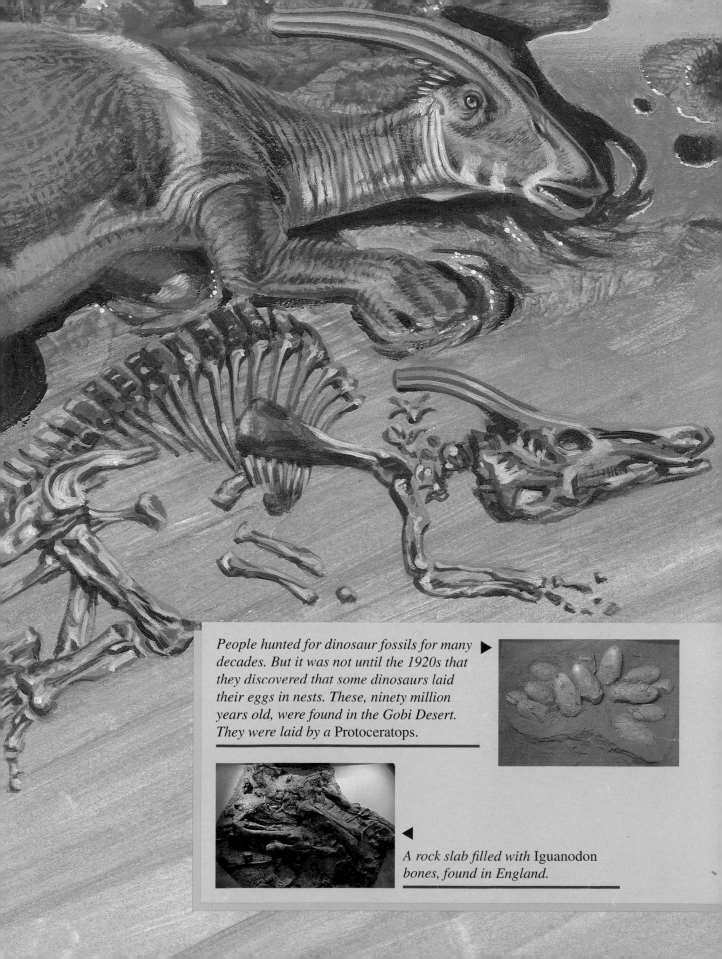

People hunted for dinosaur fossils for many decades. But it was not until the 1920s that they discovered that some dinosaurs laid their eggs in nests. These, ninety million years old, were found in the Gobi Desert. They were laid by a Protoceratops.

A rock slab filled with Iguanodon bones, found in England.

Scientists determined from the location of fossils in the layers of sedimentary stone that dinosaurs died out quite suddenly.

Sudden Death

Another fact scientists have learned about dinosaurs was that they died out quite suddenly. Scientists knew this because of the way dinosaur fossils lay in the ground. These fossils always appeared in certain layers of a type of stone called *sedimentary rock*. Above these layers were no dinosaur remains at all.

Scientists knew approximately how old each layer was. Therefore, they could tell how long ago the last dinosaurs lived. The evidence from rocks around the world showed that about sixty-five million years ago the dinosaurs abruptly became extinct. With the dinosaurs gone, mammals were free to roam as they wanted. They swiftly increased in size and variety and became the dominant life forms on the planet.

How did so many varied and successful dinosaurs disappear so suddenly and so completely? This has been one of the greatest mysteries of science for more than 150 years.

CHAPTER 2

Mystery of the Mass Deaths

Beginning in the days of Gideon Mantell and Richard Owen, enthusiastic researchers looked for clues to the mystifying mass deaths of the dinosaurs. Scientists began to offer theories to explain their deaths and the disappearance of other Mesozoic animals and plants. Mesozoic is the name of the time when dinosaurs lived—about 65 to 225 million years ago. One of the first ideas was proposed in the 1800s. It was that mammals crept into dinosaur nests and ate the eggs. For a time the image of warm-blooded mammals outwitting and finally defeating their huge cold-blooded enemies was popular.

Most researchers eventually decided this explanation was not very satisfactory. For one thing, mammals in Mesozoic times were small and not very numerous. There probably were not enough of them to kill so many dinosaurs so quickly. Also, mammals existed alongside dinosaurs for millions of years. Why, after all that time, would mammals suddenly start eating dinosaur eggs? The egg-eating idea could not explain the extinction of plants and ocean reptiles either.

Another theory claimed that the dinosaurs died out because their brains were too small. According to this view, as their bodies got bigger and bigger, their brains stayed the same size. The *Apatosaurus* seemed a perfect illustration of this idea. It weighed up to thirty tons. But its brain was only about the size of an orange. No one believed such a small brain could efficiently operate such a large body. Scientists thought the beasts eventually became too stupid. They could not adapt to change, so they perished, or died.

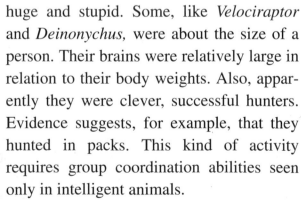

Apatosaurus, above, was very large, but had a small brain. And Deinonychus (below) though much smaller, had a very large brain.

However, most scientists refused to accept this explanation. They pointed out that dinosaurs managed to survive with small brains for 160 million years. Also, not all dinosaurs were huge and stupid. Some, like *Velociraptor* and *Deinonychus,* were about the size of a person. Their brains were relatively large in relation to their body weights. Also, apparently they were clever, successful hunters. Evidence suggests, for example, that they hunted in packs. This kind of activity requires group coordination abilities seen only in intelligent animals.

Also, like the egg-eating theory, the small-brain proposal did not explain all the extinctions. Said dinosaur expert Helen Sattler in *The Illustrated Dinosaur Dictionary,* "Stupidity couldn't have caused the plants . . . to become extinct."

Disease and Starvation

A third theory suggested that the dinosaurs died from disease. Supposedly, a terrible plague, or disease, swept the world, killing all the dinosaurs. As some of the beasts died in agony, others feasted on them. Those eating the diseased meat caught and spread the plague. But some scientists thought disease was not the answer. They pointed out that it is unlikely one disease could affect every type of dinosaur. Also, why would the disease have killed most reptiles, yet allow some, like crocodiles and turtles, to survive? And, once again, the extinction of so many plants had to be considered. Thousands of species of plants became extinct during the same period. A plague that struck down dinosaurs would have had no effect at all on plants.

Mass starvation was another idea proposed to explain the dinosaurs' disappearance. The plant-eating dinosaurs ate mostly soft ferns and flowering plants. Near the end of the

Diplodocus, believed to be the longest dinosaur, had a very small head and jaws that cause scientists to wonder how the creature managed to eat enough to stay alive.

Mesozoic Era, these types of plants decreased in number, and hard grasses increased. Some scientists thought the herbivorous dinosaurs did not have the kinds of teeth necessary to chew the new grasses. Scientists imagined the massive beasts desperately wandering around the countryside, searching for plants they could chew and swallow. Each of the big dinosaurs needed hundreds of pounds of food a day. When their food became scarce, they slowly died of starvation. The carnivores lived by eating the herbivores. So when the herbivores died out, the carnivores starved, too.

Those who support this idea also point out that some dinosaurs may have had very specialized diets. When the food they were used to disappeared, they could not adjust to eating

Although Apatosaurus, *center rear, was huge, this dinosaur was a plant eater and often was attacked by* Tyrannosaurus rex, *left, and other meat eaters who were leaner and meaner.*

something else. Says James Hopson, of the University of Chicago, "If they ate mainly one plant, just as the koala bear lives on eucalyptus, they would be in trouble if that plant were no longer available."

Opponents of this theory say it does not explain how the large oceangoing reptiles died out. They did not eat ferns, grasses, or any other plants that grew on land. They were like giant eating machines patrolling the waters. They devoured the abundant fish, squid, and other marine life. Also, the theory does not account for the plant extinctions themselves. Nearly half of the species of land plants perished quite suddenly at the end of the Mesozoic Era. By contrast, the appearance of grasses was a relatively gradual process.

Were Dinosaurs Warm-Blooded?

Reptiles are cold-blooded; they receive heat from their surroundings. To warm up, they lie in the sun. Crocodiles rest on warm riverbanks, snakes bask on sunny rocks, and turtles perch on floating logs. To cool off, these animals retreat into the shade. Mammals are warm-blooded. Their bodies produce heat on the inside. Scientists consider dinosaurs to be reptiles and, therefore, cold-blooded. This would mean they would not be able to survive a sudden, permanent cooling of their tropical climate.

However, some evidence suggests that dinosaurs were warm-blooded like mammals. Mammals and birds walk erect on two legs. Dr. Robert Bakker and other scientists say that warm-blooded mammals and birds can walk this way because they have complicated and powerful hearts. Reptiles' hearts are simpler, and reptiles move close to the ground, on stomach or four legs. Many dinosaurs, like mammals, walked erect. Bakker thinks this means dinosaurs may have been warm-blooded, too.

Also, say Bakker and his colleagues, many dinosaurs appear to have been very active. They ran and leapt long distances. Normally only warm-blooded animals perform such activity.

If dinosaurs were warm-blooded, many of them could have adapted to colder weather. This means that climate change is not a very likely reason for dinosaur extinction.

This painting shows two lively, battling dinosaurs. Robert Bakker and some other scientists believe that only warm-blooded animals are likely to be so active.

Changes in Climate

One of the most popular extinction theories of the early twentieth century was that changes in climate killed the dinosaurs.

The weather in the Mesozoic Era was tropical. It was hot and moist year-round across most of the world. Palm trees, giant ferns, and dense rain forests thrived in most of the lowland areas. Supposedly this tropical weather cooled off rapidly in the late Mesozoic. The north and south polar ice caps began to grow. The air and water around the world got colder. But the dinosaurs were cold-blooded. They could not produce their own internal body heat as mammals do. The great reptiles relied instead on heat from direct sunlight or tropical air to keep them warm. They could not cope with the sudden cooling trend in the weather.

Many paleontologists argued that the climate changed gradually, not suddenly. They said it took many thousands of years for the world's overall temperature to drop a single degree. So even cold-blooded dinosaurs would have had plenty of time to migrate to warmer areas or to adapt. Besides, said opponents of the theory, many large reptiles did manage to survive. Dinosaur expert Edwin Colbert asked, "If the crocodiles could make it, why not some of the dinosaurs?"

Most scientists think dinosaurs were most at home in a tropical climate (top). Would they be unable to adapt to a sudden change—to the coming of an Ice Age?

Scientists offered many other explanations for the extinctions. Each proposal explained how some of the dinosaurs and other living things might have died out. But none of the theories satisfied most of the paleontologists. Nothing on earth seemed to explain how so many successful species could have died so suddenly all over the planet.

CHAPTER 3

Disaster from Beyond Earth

The stars were shining brightly on a cold, clear evening in 1956. Joseph Shlovsky was preparing for a night's work. He was one of the Soviet Union's leading astronomers. He was working at an observatory near the northern coast of the Black Sea. He had just left a gathering of scientists. They had discussed dinosaur extinction. Shlovsky began developing some photographs taken the night before. They showed gases floating in space. An ancient supernova explosion had caused the gases. A *supernova* is the violent explosion of a star. Suddenly Shlovsky had a new and exciting idea. What if the dinosaurs had died from the effects of a supernova?

Shlovsky realized that none of the earth-based theories, such as changes in climate, and planetwide disease, seemed to explain the late Mesozoic mass deaths very well. So, he reasoned, perhaps something *extraterrestrial,* or from beyond the earth, caused the disaster. A supernova is one of the most destructive events in all of nature. It seemed a likely possibility. A supernova occurs when a large star that is several times the size of the sun becomes unstable and explodes. The explosion releases a huge blast of energy. This energy takes the forms of light, heat, and powerful radioactivity.

Shlovsky believed a nearby star may have become a supernova about sixty-five million years ago. If so, the explosion would have showered the earth with dangerous radiation. Many animals would have died immediately. Others would have died later from cancer. Or they would have lost their ability to reproduce. Such a disaster would also have destroyed many plant species.

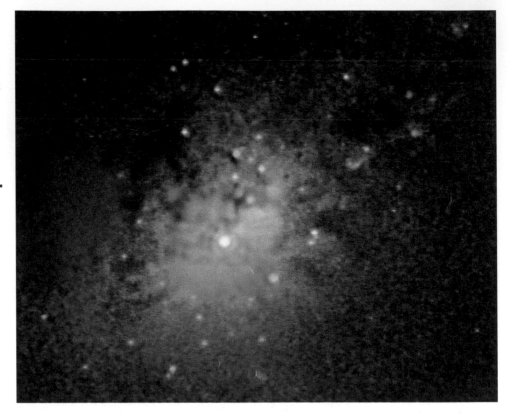

This photograph of a supernova was taken by NASA's Hubble Space Telescope in 1992. Some scientists think radiation from a supernova showered the earth sixty-five million years ago and killed the dinosaurs.

But how could 30 percent of the plants and animals on earth have survived the effects of the supernova? Shlovsky suggested that mammals and other small creatures burrowed underground. Layers of dirt protected them. Some crocodiles and turtles buried themselves in mud, so their species also survived. Dinosaurs, on the other hand, had nowhere to hide, so they became extinct.

Many scientists were not convinced by the supernova theory. They said that such a catastrophe would leave "fingerprints," or physical evidence, in the rocks of the earth's crust. A nearby supernova would leave traces of radioactive elements, such as *plutonium,* in the rocks. Such traces might be uneven and distributed in random areas. Still, they would be easy to detect. Researchers found no plutonium in the rock and clay layers that matched the time of the extinctions. Even though most scientists did not accept Shlovsky's theory, it was important. It introduced the idea that something from beyond the earth killed the dinosaurs.

Collision!

This idea surfaced again in the 1970s. Luis Alvarez was a Nobel Prize-winning scientist. He was conducting a routine examination of rock layers from the time of the extinctions. To his surprise he found concentrations of the element iridium that were thirty times higher than normal. *Iridium* is a dark heavy metal. It is very rare on the earth's surface. Most of the earth's iridium sank to the planet's core long ago. But the element is fairly common in extraterrestrial objects such as meteors, asteroids, and comets. This fact led Alvarez to propose an unusual and dramatic theory. He suggested that an asteroid or other large cosmic body collided with the earth. The collision,

Dr. Luis Alvarez (below, left) and his son Dr. Walter Alvarez were the first to make popular the idea that a comet may have killed the dinosaurs.

said Alvarez, caused a massive explosion. It showered the earth with debris, including iridium. He explained that the collision could have led to the great mass deaths, including those of the dinosaurs.

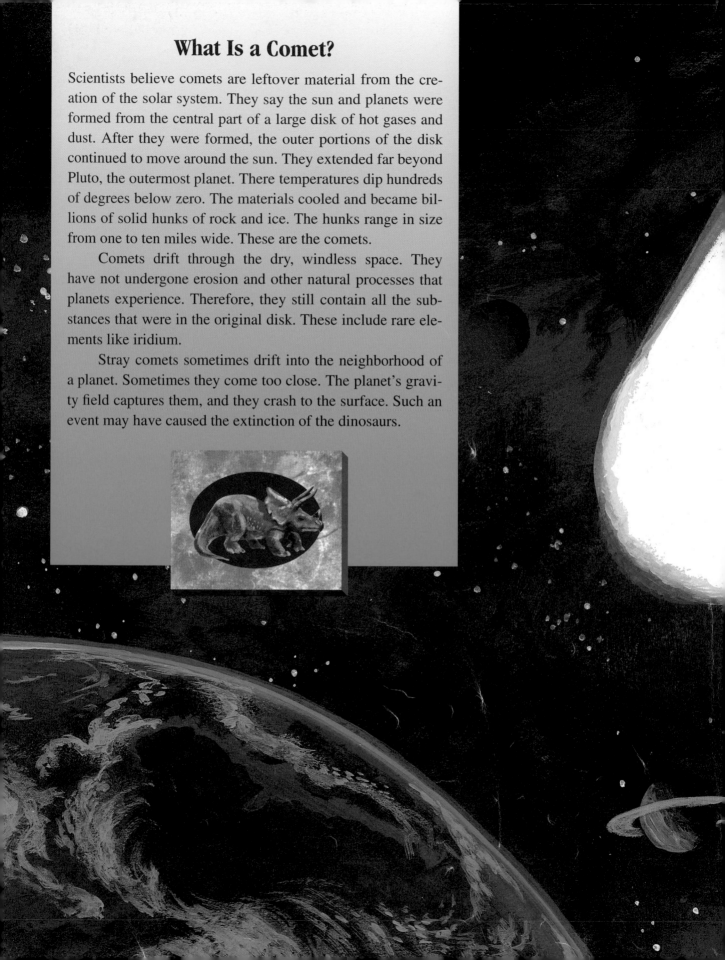

What Is a Comet?

Scientists believe comets are leftover material from the creation of the solar system. They say the sun and planets were formed from the central part of a large disk of hot gases and dust. After they were formed, the outer portions of the disk continued to move around the sun. They extended far beyond Pluto, the outermost planet. There temperatures dip hundreds of degrees below zero. The materials cooled and became billions of solid hunks of rock and ice. The hunks range in size from one to ten miles wide. These are the comets.

Comets drift through the dry, windless space. They have not undergone erosion and other natural processes that planets experience. Therefore, they still contain all the substances that were in the original disk. These include rare elements like iridium.

Stray comets sometimes drift into the neighborhood of a planet. Sometimes they come too close. The planet's gravity field captures them, and they crash to the surface. Such an event may have caused the extinction of the dinosaurs.

A comet starts as a nucleus, or core, of frozen gases and dust. Astronomer Fred Whipple says it is something like a "dirty snowball." As it nears the sun, the gases heat up. They create a glowing cloud, called a coma, around the nucleus. The comet also develops a dust-and-gas tail that may be millions of miles long.

Alvarez's son Walter, also a scientist, agreed with the collision theory. The two men, aided by other researchers, eagerly began searching for more iridium. They soon found unusually rich deposits of the metal in many areas of the world. To the scientists' delight, these deposits always occurred in the rock layers dated at about sixty-five million years ago.

According to the Alvarezes, the asteroid or comet that ended the Mesozoic Era was six or more miles in diameter. Traveling at the incredible speed of forty thousand miles per hour, it smashed into the earth. The tremendous impact carved out a crater at least one hundred miles across. It threw up a huge cloud of dust and rock particles. The explosion also caused violent earthquakes. It ignited forest fires all over the planet. The smoke from the fires combined with the dust from the impact. They formed a thick, dark cloud in the upper part of the atmosphere.

An asteroid smashing into Earth could create a crater one hundred miles wide, cause earthquakes and forest fires, and produce a cloud of dust and rock particles so dense it could block the sun for days, weeks, or years.

This cloud, said the Alvarezes, proved to be deadly to life on earth. It blocked most of the incoming sunlight for many months, perhaps even a few years. Even in the middle of the daytime it seemed like night. With the sunlight gone, temperatures suddenly dropped to below freezing. Most plants, which require sunlight to live, withered. Since plants were the main food source of herbivorous dinosaurs, big plant eaters like *Apatosaurus* died within days or weeks. When the plant eaters died, carnivores like *Tyrannosaurus* and *Deinonychus* had nothing to eat. So they perished, too.

Some small creatures, like mammals, managed to survive the catastrophe. For one thing, they could descend into their burrows to escape the cold. And they were scavengers. They could live off the dead bodies of dinosaurs and other animals until the sunlight returned.

Many scientists felt that the collision theory explained the sudden mass extinctions very well. It accounted for the death of the dinosaurs and other large reptiles. It also explained the destruction of many kinds of plants. In addition, it showed how mammals and other living things could have survived extinction.

Some scientists were not convinced. They insisted that such a giant impact would have left a very noticeable crater. No one could find any large craters dating from the time of the extinctions. The researchers had only some of the pieces in the cosmic catastrophe puzzle. Until someone found the mysterious impact crater, the puzzle could not be completed.

CHAPTER 4

Clues to Cosmic Collision

If the dinosaurs died from a cosmic collision, where is the crater that would have been carved into the earth? Luis and Walter Alvarez and other scientists say it may no longer be visible. In fact, objects from space have hit the earth many times. But very few impact craters can be seen on earth's land surfaces. This is because of erosion, the wearing down of the land by wind, rain, and sun. The process slowly erases and fills in craters and other depressions. Therefore only the most recent impact craters are visible. One example is Barringer Crater, located near Winslow, Arizona. It is nearly a mile across and six hundred feet deep. It formed when a meteor crashed into the desert about twenty-five thousand years ago.

Another possibility is that the extraterrestrial killer plunged into the ocean. Since water covers more than 70 percent of the planet's surface, this is more likely than a land strike. The impact would have created a huge crater on the ocean floor.

Like the land surfaces, the ocean floors also change over the course of time. Heat from the earth's molten core, or hot, liquid center, constantly rises. It melts many of the rocks directly beneath the earth's solid crust. Some of this hot liquefied rock oozes up through cracks in the areas of the ocean where the crust is thinnest. It cools and becomes solid. Then the new rock forces the ocean bottom to expand and slowly move outward. Eventually these moving surfaces grind back down into the earth. They turn to liquid once more. In this way the ocean floors are continually recycled. It is possible that this process destroyed the impact crater during the millions of years since the fatal collision.

Caribbean Rocks

Continual changes on the land and the ocean floor at first made the possibility of finding the sixty-five-million-year-old crater seem unlikely. Yet scientists eventually found evidence that might be proof of the cosmic intruder. In 1988 Alan Hildebrand and William Boynton of the University of Arizona decided to search for signs of ancient tsunamis. *Tsunamis* are huge ocean waves, also known as tidal waves. They sometimes occur as the result of earthquakes or volcanic eruptions. Hildebrand and Boynton reasoned that a comet impact in the sea would produce gigantic tsunamis, perhaps as much as three miles high. These waves would carry rocks from the ocean floor and deposit them in piles on the land surfaces.

The two scientists studied rock layers in Mexico, Cuba, and the southern United States. These areas border the Caribbean Sea. The men immediately made a thrilling discovery. Each area had a layer containing piles of boulders that were different from the rocks above and below them. The

A tidal wave, or tsunami, during the Mesozoic Era, deposits countless tons of rocks and debris across the land.

boulders did not seem to belong in the area where they were found. Further examination showed that the boulders were the same kinds normally found on the floor of the Caribbean. Could this sea be where the dinosaur's "death star" fell? After studying maps of the floor of the Caribbean, researchers believe that they have found signs of a large, ancient crater.

Some scientists believe the extraterrestrial object may not have fallen in the Caribbean. They think it could have struck some other spot on the ocean floor in a place where the earth's crust was unusually thin. The collision might have shattered the crust. This would expose the red-hot liquefied rock beneath. Over the course of thousands of years, these hot masses could have filled in the crater and then continued to ooze up from below. The molten rock would have formed a mound that grew into a huge underwater mountain. Eventually this mountain would have reached the ocean's surface. It would have created a volcanic island like Hawaii.

Volcanoes work under the ocean much as they do on land—spewing out lava, flame, and other substances. A volcano can erase all traces of a meteor crater. That may be why scientists have had difficulty finding a crater from the comet some believe killed the dinosaurs.

Are Birds Living Dinosaurs?

Scientists call the first known bird *Archaeopteryx*. It lived alongside dinosaurs in the Mesozoic Era. For many years scientists thought *Archaeopteryx* and dinosaurs were not related. However, they now know that *Archaeopteryx*'s bone structure was nearly the same as that of the small dinosaur *Compsognathus*. Researchers say some small dinosaurs might have developed feathers for insulation against the cold. Later they might have adapted the feathers for flight. If so, today's birds are the living descendants of dinosaurs.

What If the Dinosaurs Had Not Died?

In 1982 two Canadian scientists tried to answer this question. Dale A. Russell and Ron Sequin suggested what might have happened if the dinosaurs had continued to evolve, or develop. They chose the dinosaur *Stenonychosaurus* as a model. This small dinosaur had a good-sized brain. It also had opposable thumbs, which meant that it could grasp objects as people can. After millions of years, the scientists say, *Stenonychosaurus* could have evolved into a creature with humanlike intelligence. They named their reptile-person Dinosauroid. If the Dinosauroid had evolved, they say, mammals would not have become dominant. Human beings would never have developed.

This painting shows the kind of impact that would be made if an object five hundred miles in diameter struck the earth. The meteorite that caused the huge Barringer Crater in Arizona (left) is believed to have been only a fraction of this size.

In 1981 scientists Fred Whipple and Isaac Asimov suggested an island that might have been created by the object that killed the dinosaurs: Iceland. The island of Iceland in the northern Atlantic Ocean is one of the most active volcanic areas in the world. The island is only about the size of the state of Kentucky. Yet it has more than two hundred volcanoes and over six hundred major hot springs. To fit the time frame of the collision theory, Iceland would have to be considerably younger than sixty-five million years. And this is indeed the case. Scientists say that Iceland rose from the ocean only during the last few million years. In addition, says Asimov, the pattern of iridium layers seems to support the idea that Iceland was the impact site. For example, iridium levels in Italy, far from Iceland, are about 30 times higher than normal. Levels of iridium in Denmark, much closer to Iceland, are 160 times higher.

Disagreement About Collision

Despite favorable evidence, scientists do not yet universally accept the collision theory. For instance, paleontologist Robert Bakker insists the extinction of the dinosaurs happened gradually, not suddenly. He argues that close examination of the earth layers proves this. The layers containing fossils show that dinosaur species died out a few at a time, not all at once, he says. Bakker believes migrating animals carried disease parasites. These slowly killed the dinosaurs.

But a majority of researchers say the collision theory is the most convincing explanation proposed so far. It is the only theory that explains most or all of the mysteries surrounding the extinctions. And each year more evidence comes to light in support of it.

Unsolved Mystery

Part of the appeal of the collision theory is that it shows how the earth is a small part of a larger cosmic order. Our tiny planet hurtles through an ever-changing, often violent universe. And life on earth, including the human race, is not immune to this violence.

Perhaps someday new evidence will come to light about the catastrophe that ended the long reign of the dinosaurs. This evidence may prove once and for all how these unique and fascinating creatures met their end. In the meantime, the mystery surrounding that end remains officially unsolved.

This photo shows the great galaxy in Andromeda. It is similar in many respects to our Milky Way Galaxy, but it is two million light years (or about 12,000,000,000,000,000,000 miles) distant. The galaxies, the planets, and humans are all tiny inhabitants of the vast and mysterious universe—and so were the dinosaurs.

Glossary

Anatosaurus: Also known as *Trachodon;* thirty feet long, weighing about three to four tons; plant eater, with a flat duck-like bill.

Apatosaurus: Also known as *Brontosaurus;* seventy feet long, weighing up to thirty tons; plant eater, with a long neck and tail and a tiny head.

Archaeopteryx: The first bird; one to three feet long, with feathers; probably ate insects.

asteroid: A hunk of rock or metal that floats in space; usually located between the orbits of the planets Mars and Jupiter.

Brachiosaurus: Seventy feet long, weighing up to eighty tons; plant eater, with a long neck and a small crested head.

carnivore: A meat-eating animal.

comet: A mass of rock and ice left over from the formation of the solar system, usually located beyond the orbit of Pluto.

Compsognathus: About one to two feet long, weighing four or five pounds; ate insects and small reptiles and mammals; ran on its hind feet.

cosmic: Having to do with the cosmos, or universe, usually used to describe things in outer space.

Deinonychus: Eight feet long, weighing 175 to 200 pounds; meat eater and a pack hunter; ran on its hind feet, each of which had a sharp, curved spike for slashing its prey.

dinosaur: An ancient, extinct land reptile that walked with its legs directly beneath its body. By contrast, the legs of lizards, crocodiles, turtles, and other reptiles project outward from their sides.

evolve: To change in physical form slowly over the course of thousands or millions of years.

extinction: The death of a whole group of living things.

extraterrestrial: Coming from beyond the earth.

fossils: The hardened remains of plants and animals.

herbivore: A plant-eating animal.

*Iguanodon***:** Twenty-five feet long, weighing five tons; plant eater with five-fingered hands; the first dinosaur ever found.

iridium: A rare metal found mainly in extraterrestrial objects such as meteors and comets.

mammal: A warm-blooded, hairy animal that bears its young alive and nurses them with milk from its mammary glands; for example, a rabbit, cat, or human being.

Mesozoic Era: A period in the earth's history that lasted from about 225 to 65 million years ago.

meteor: A hunk of rock or metal that floats through space.

Nobel Prize: A famous honor given each year to people who have made great discoveries or achievements.

orbit: The path taken by an object in space as it moves around another object; for example, the earth orbits the sun.

paleontologist: A scientist who studies fossils, or ancient life forms.

paleontology: The study of fossils, or ancient life forms.

plutonium: A dangerous radioactive element often used as fuel for nuclear reactors.

predator: An animal that preys on other animals, stalking, killing, and feeding on them.

*Protoceratops***:** Six feet long, weighing eight hundred to nine hundred pounds; plant eater, with a large head and a curved beak.

radioactive: Giving off radiation, which is a stream of quick-moving microscopic particles that can sometimes be dangerous to living things.

reptile: A normally cold-blooded, hairless animal that bears its young by laying eggs; for example, a turtle, alligator, or snake.

scavenger: An animal that eats food left behind by other animals.

species: A specific kind of animal or plant.

star: A large ball of gas that gives off heat and light because of nuclear reactions in its core; for example, the sun.

Stegosaurus: Twenty-five feet long, weighing three to six tons; plant eater, with a tiny head and a double row of bony plates running down its back.

Stenonychosaurus: About six feet long, weighing 150 to 180 pounds; meat eater; ran rapidly on its hind legs; a pack hunter; large brained, with good vision; thought by scientists to have been the most intelligent dinosaur.

supernova: The gigantic blast of an exploding star.

tsunami: A giant sea wave, sometimes called a tidal wave, although such waves have nothing to do with the tides.

Tyrannosaurus rex: Fifty feet long, eighteen to twenty feet tall, weighing six tons; meat eater, with huge jaws filled with daggerlike teeth; ran on its hind legs, although probably slowly because of its great size; the largest predator that ever lived.

Velociraptor: Five to six feet tall, weighing 100 to 150 pounds; meat eater, probably a pack hunter, with sharp claws and teeth; ran on its hind legs.

For Further Reading

Isaac Asimov, *Counting the Eons.* New York: Avon Books, 1983.

Robin Bates and Cheryl Simon, *The Dinosaurs and the Dark Star.* New York: Macmillan Publishers, 1985.

Donald Goldsmith, *Nemesis: The Death Star and Other Theories of Mass Extinction.* New York: Berkeley Books, 1985.

Christopher Lampton, *Dinosaurs and the Age of Reptiles.* New York: Watts, 1983.

Don Nardo, *Gravity: The Universal Force.* San Diego, CA: Lucent Books, 1990.

Gregory S. Paul, "Life Styles of the Big and Hungry," *Science Digest,* April/May 1990.

Helen Roney Sattler, *The Illustrated Dinosaur Dictionary.* New York: Lothrop, 1983.

Peter Zallinger, *Dinosaurs and Other Archosaurs.* New York: Random House, 1986.

Works Consulted

Robert T. Bakker, *The Dinosaur Heresies*. New York: William Morrow and Company, 1986.

Alan J. Charig, *A New Look at the Dinosaurs*. New York: Mayflower Books, 1979.

John R. Horner, *Digging Dinosaurs*. New York: Workman Publishing, 1988.

Kenneth J. Hsu, *The Great Dying*. New York: Ballantine Books, 1986.

David Norman, *The Illustrated Encyclopedia of Dinosaurs*. New York: Crescent Books, 1985.

Peter Roop and Connie Roop, *Dinosaurs*. St. Paul, MN: Greenhaven Press, 1988.

Tom Waters, "Cretaceous Splashdown," *Discover,* September 1990.

John Noble Wilford, *The Riddle of the Dinosaur.* New York: Vintage Books, 1985.

Index

Picture Credits

About the Author

Don Nardo is an actor, makeup artist, film director, composer, and teacher, as well as a writer. As an actor he has appeared in more than fifty stage productions, including several Shakespeare plays. He has also worked before or behind the camera in twenty films. Several of his musical compositions, including a young person's version of *The War of the Worlds,* and the oratorio *Richard III,* have been performed by regional orchestras. Mr. Nardo's writing credits include short stories, articles, and more than forty books, including *Lasers: Humanity's Magic Light, The Irish Potato Famine, Exercise, Anxiety, and Phobias,* and *The Mexican-American War.* Among his other writings are an episode of ABC's "Spenser: For Hire" and the award-winning screenplay *The Bet.* Mr. Nardo lives with his wife Christine on Cape Cod, Massachusetts.